A Place of My Own
to
Give God Glory

Forty Days of Inspirational Devotions

for

Reflection and Meditation

Gwendolyn Wilson Diggs, EdD

iUniverse, Inc.
Bloomington

A Place of My Own to Give God Glory
Forty Days of Inspirational Devotions for Reflection and Meditation

iUniverse books may be ordered through booksellers or by contacting:

iUniverse
1663 Liberty Drive
Bloomington, IN 47403
www.iuniverse.com
1-800-Authors (1-800-288-4677)

Photographs © 2011 Gwendolyn Wilson Diggs

All scripture references are from the Holy Bible: The Kings James Study Bible. (previously published as The Liberty Annotated Study Bible, The Annotated Study Bible), King James Version, 1988. Nashville: Thomas Nelson Publishers.

ISBN: 978-1-4502-9653-3 (pbk)
ISBN: 978-1-4502-9655-7 (cloth)
ISBN: 978-1-4502-9654-0 (ebk)

Library of Congress Control Number: 2011902224

Printed in the United States of America

iUniverse rev. date: 05/05/2011

To my husband,
Darryl S. Diggs Sr., who loves me and understands my need to stay on my knees.

To my children,
Darryl Jr., Jordan, and Ardella,
who God loaned me to love and instruct in the ways of Christ.

To my parents,
Elder Willie Wilson Sr. and
Missionary Morliner Danley Wilson,
who trained me as a child to follow Christ.

To my sisters
Jean and Rena,
who join me in every endeavor, both natural and spiritual.

To my brothers
Willie, Everett, Joseph, Jonathan, and Christopher,
who I know love me and I love more.

To my parents,
brothers, and sisters in Christ—continue to
GIVE GOD GLORY!

That I may publish with the voice of thanksgiving,
and tell of all thy wondrous works.
Psalms 26:7

Contents

Acknowledgments

"In all thy ways acknowledge Him, and He shall direct thy paths" (Proverbs 3:6). Putting God first and seeking His face is the inspiration and guiding force for these devotions.

Thank you to my family and friends for allowing me to share my thoughts, for reading my devotions, and for providing unconditional love and support. Having family and friends who believe as I do, that all things are possible, contributes to my constant motivation to write about the awesomeness of God.

A special thank you to Alice Perrey, professor at Saint Louis Christian College in Florissant, Missouri, for your friendship and support.

Preface

The Lord said, "Spread My word and proclaim the gospel of Christ."

All my life, I have marveled at the talents of others. The mesmerizing saxophone player performing before large congregations, the soul-stirring soloist causing people to stand and rejoice, and the preachers and missionaries standing before a crowd flawlessly delivering God's inspiring word have caused me to wonder what happened to me. I come from a large family that is gifted musically. It's no secret that I can't carry a tune. This fact has been shared candidly by family and friends over the years. However, I have made several enjoyable attempts to play the saxophone and the clarinet.

With limited musical talent, I screamed to the Lord and asked what do You want me to do, show me my purpose. This was my constant song and prayer. I would repeat over and over in my head and heart, *I don't know my purpose.* Others around me were moving forward, exercising their God-given gifts. Everyone continued to tell me that I knew what I was to do, but really, I didn't have a clue. I asked them to tell me, but they would not share what God placed in their spirits. They would always say, "It's better to let the Lord lead and guide you." I became increasingly frustrated because I never seemed to see or hear what God was saying.

Again, while attending a Saturday prayer chat meeting, I was told that I knew what God wanted me to do. Everyone in the room was praying and seeking the Lord. I got so frustrated that I began to go deep into seeking God's face with my routine question and asked Him, "What do you want me to do?" I was physically doubled over in the spirit when the Lord spoke to me and said, "Spread my Word and proclaim the gospel of Christ." I stopped praying and started crying. After hearing His voice, I did not know how to act upon His words. Not knowing the next steps to take, I continued to ask God how to spread His Word and how to proclaim the gospel of Christ. Each day became a day that I would live and speak to someone about Christ. It was several years later that the Lord revealed to me that I was to spread His Word and proclaim the gospel of Christ through sharing personal experiences in devotional writings.

Spreading God's Word and proclaiming the gospel of Christ is the aim of *A Place of My Own to Give God Glory*. The devotions are the inspired Word of God and include personal accounts of my life experiences. Without a doubt, each step of the journey to write these devotions left me spiritually immersed in the warmth of God's love.

Let this devotional book be your guide to increase your faith and spiritual walk. Use the journal pages to reflect on the devotional reading as you mediate on the Word of God. Your daily walk with the Lord will command your day and show you how to give God glory.

A Place of My Own

But thou, when thou prayest, enter into thy closet, and when thou hast shut thy door, pray to thy Father which is in secret; and thy Father which seeth in secret shall reward thee openly.—Matthew 6:6

I always desired a place to steal away to pray, a sacred prayer place to call my own. Before we moved, I would go into the bathroom, living room, or any room to privately seek God's face. I would bend down beside the bed in a fetal position so that my husband would not see me if he woke up. That way, the sound of the door would not wake him, nor would he see me on my knees. Nevertheless, each time I attempted to pray, I seemed to interfere with someone by waking them up or just by being in the way, depending on the time of the day.

In this dedicated place to meet God in prayer that I wanted, I would surround myself with everything that I needed to let God know that I was sincere about serving Him and doing His work. I would say yes to God and listen to Him say yes to me. Yes, He will do it; yes, He will give me the desires of my heart; and yes, it is done. I agree with Psalms 55:17, which says, "Evening, and morning, and at noon, will I pray, and cry aloud: And he shall hear my voice." Five years after purchasing a piece of land, we began to build on the property. In that time I had written down on a yellow piece of paper what I wanted in a house, including my very own personal space.

The décor of my personal room had to be red for two reasons: the blood of Christ and Delta Sigma Theta Sorority, Inc. To complete the room I just wanted a red chair. I knew I did not have the money to buy the chairs that I had priced at various furniture stores. I made my request known to God and moved on to other things.

One Saturday, my husband and I attended a track meet for my daughter. On the way home, I asked him to stop by a furniture warehouse that was having a sale. We looked around the store and found it was truly a sale.

Early bargain hunters seemed to have cleaned the place out. The prices of some of the remaining items appeared to be a steal. My husband kept saying, "We don't need and we can't afford to buy anything." I gravitated toward the red leather chairs. All of the chairs were cheaper than I had priced elsewhere but were still over my budget. I kept looking around the store at rugs, tables, and so forth. When it was time to leave, God led me back down the same aisle of chairs. I stopped in front of one of the softest oversized red leather chairs that I had ever seen. I looked at the tag and looked at it again. The tag read ninety-nine dollars. My husband said, "Stand there." He went to get a sales lady to verify the price. The chair was definitely mine. It fit perfectly in my vehicle. Just thinking and talking about the chair makes me emotional, because it completes my spiritual place.

Sometimes I kneel by the chair, sometimes I sit to read, sometimes I lean down at the foot of the chair, and in times of crying out to God, it catches my tears. The red chair reminds me of the scripture, "Come to me all ye that labor and are heavy laden and I will give you rest" (Matthew 11:28). God is complete. He makes me complete. He promises to help me and to be with me. I thank God for my place of worship and my chair. I told my son to sit in the chair and be blessed. I had to bring the computer to the chair to complete this writing.

This morning I sat in my space with tears in my eyes, thanking God for doing it. I stand in awe each day of the glory of God and what only God can provide. He is an awesome God. When I asked for an extraordinary home, God made just that. Each time I think about how extraordinary the house is, He whispers, "You haven't seen anything yet." When God whispered to me that everything that I need would come through my knees, that was what He meant. There is peace, renewal, and joy when I fall on my knees in front of the red chair. I need no preliminaries or an introduction into my relationship with God at the red chair; the purpose is understood. He meets me at the red chair. Find a place to call your own.

My Prayer:

_____

_____

_____

_____

_____

His Voice:

_____

_____

_____

_____

_____

My Action:

_____

_____

_____

_____

_____

Day 2

Believe

I have called thee by thy name; thou art mine. When thou passest through the waters, I will be with thee; and through the rivers, they shall not overflow thee: when thou walkest through the fire, thou shalt not be burned; neither shall the flame kindle upon thee. Ye are my witnesses, saith the LORD, and my servant whom I have chosen: that ye may know and bwelieve *me, and understand that I am he: before me there was no God formed, neither shall there be after me.* —Isaiah 43:1–2, 10

We must remember to step back in order to step forward. Stepping back allows us to have a better perspective on where God wants us to go, or should I say where He wants to lead us. Often, we busy ourselves with routines, projects, meetings, and deadlines without stopping to give God glory or ask for advice on how to proceed with the tasks at hand. Start each day by asking God to organize your thoughts and your day. We must strengthen our faith in God and the way we acknowledge His promises to experience our greatest natural and spiritual success.

One morning, I knelt down to pray and ended belly-up on the floor with my arms extended as the spirit of the Lord grabbed my heart. What was vivid during my prayer time was the image of the position of Christ on the cross and the emotions I felt from the pain and suffering He endured for our sins. There I met Him to say, "Thank you," and to give God glory.

I encourage you to think about changing positions while praying. Try lying prostrate before the Lord to pray. Extend your arms to form a cross with your body and begin to call out His name. Ask God to order your steps so that you might work and walk more effectively and efficiently for Him. God will guide us as we seek to be more productive in order to meet the demands of the day. As you go through your day, say and do everything for His glory. Believe that He will reward you if you seek Him with your whole heart. Expect God's favor to be upon your life every day. You are personally chosen by God, and He is with you always.

My Prayer:

_____

_____

_____

_____

_____

His Voice:

_____

_____

_____

_____

_____

My Action:

_____

_____

_____

_____

_____

Be a Vessel

But the Lord said unto him, Go thy way: for he is a chosen vessel unto me, to bear my name before the Gentiles, and kings, and the children of Israel: For I will show him how great things he must suffer for my name's sake.—Acts 9:15–16

The human body is a vessel that wears a "Made by God" label. Manufactured garments come with specific cleaning instructions. Some clothing requires hot, warm, or cold water for proper cleaning. Special instructions might include dry cleaning to maintain the garment's longevity. Likewise, the vessel that God created, our bodies, comes with special instructions: wash in the blood and baptize in the Holy Spirit. God chose us to be a vessel that can be used for His glory. Special instruction for cleansing and preparing our vessels is found underneath the label "Holy Bible." The Bible gives us instructions for living a life that is free from sin.

Being a vessel for God is a commitment to serve Him by presenting our bodies as a living sacrifice that is holy and acceptable for the work that God has predestined in our lives (see Romans 12:1). Material vessels are filled and emptied to be filled again. God used Jesus as a vessel to carry and pour out His Word to the masses. In order to be used as a vessel for the Master, we must experience a pouring out to receive a filling up of the knowledge of Christ Jesus and the Holy Spirit.

Seek to live a life that is holy. Be a vessel that carries God's Word, and be an example that reflects the image of Christ for others to find hope, peace, and love. A vessel that carries gossip, envy, backbiting, and hatred needs spiritual cleansing. Let's daily prepare to be vessels that God can use to further His mission of bringing souls to Christ to gain physical, mental, emotional, and spiritual healing.

My Prayer:

_____

_____

_____

_____

_____

His Voice:

_____

_____

_____

_____

_____

My Action:

_____

_____

_____

_____

_____

Psalm 91

Benefits

Blessed [be] the Lord, who daily loadeth us with benefits, even the God of our salvation. Selah.—Psalms 68:19

When looking for employment, it is important to find a job that provides health insurance. Circumstances in life dictate the necessity for employment benefits. Accepting full-time or part-time employment determines the level of benefits you will receive. Think about all the benefits that God gives us when we make the commitment to fully employ ourselves to worship and praise His Holy name. There are awesome things that happen in our lives that only God can provide. David the psalmist said in Psalms 103:2: "Bless the LORD, O my soul and forget not all His benefits."

One of the many beauties of God is that He doesn't withhold rewards until we reach a specific level in our personal or professional lives. God provides for us daily, and He will not diminish the benefits as we grow older. He continues to provide for us throughout our lives by giving us the ultimate benefit of redemption for our sins and allowing us to serve Him. Our ultimate reward is waiting in heaven. God's blessings are given to us in His wish for us to prosper and be in good health. We should follow David's lead in Psalms 116:12 by asking, "What shall I render unto the LORD [for] all his benefits toward me?" All of the 401k plans in the world can't protect or provide for our welfare like God has promised. What you desire maybe delayed, but not denied.

We must not look to others to provide the benefits that only God can supply. At one time in my life I thought surely if I did all the right things and worked extremely hard, I would be recognized and recommended for a promotion. In the quietness of a work day the Lord spoke to me and said what I desired only He could provide. Societal norms have us believing that it is not what you know, but who you know that will get you ahead in life. Few believe that it is not what or who you know, but if you know Jesus Christ. Personally get to know Jesus Christ and allow Him to grace you daily with His benefits.

My Prayer:

_____

_____

_____

_____

_____

His Voice:

_____

_____

_____

_____

_____

My Action:

_____

_____

_____

_____

_____

Call Me

Call unto me, and I will answer thee, and show thee great and mighty things, which thou knowest not.—Jeremiah 33:3

We can't just say, "Okay, I'll call you," when the Lord says, "Call unto me." That is the biggest mistake imaginable. If a popular person (movie star, sports giant, multimillionaire guru, etc.) said, "Give me a call," we would not hesitate to put his number on speed dial. We would stumble all over ourselves trying to make the call. Our anxiety would reach new levels from the excitement. Our first words would be, "I am following up on our meeting, you asked me to give you a call." Why the urgency to get back to the individual? Do you expect that something good is going to happen because this individual asked you to call? Is it a job offer or your lucky break? The thought of receiving something keeps us focused on making sure contact is maintained. We can become a nuisance trying to make contact with the individual. Frustration can set in when someone tells us to give him a call and we cannot reach him. It could be that "call me" was just merely a way for him to move on.

God purposefully follows up with what He is going to do when you make the call. He promises to show us great and mighty things, great and mighty things that we don't even know about in our lifetime. God's power is limitless. Eyes have not seen nor have ears heard what God has for those who love Him. If you have experienced God's love know that it is just the beginning. You haven't seen anything yet. Keep calling His name. If we wait until we have done everything we want to do before we call upon the Lord, it could result in missed opportunities. God wants to do good things for all of His children. God gives us instructions to call Him with a purpose. He will not forget your name, face, or the encounter that prompted His instruction to call. He is waiting to answer the call.

My Prayer:

_____

_____

_____

_____

_____

His Voice:

_____

_____

_____

_____

_____

My Action:

_____

_____

_____

_____

_____

Delayed, Not Denied

I know thy works: behold, I have set before thee an open door, and no man can shut it: for thou hast a little strength, and hast kept my word, and hast not denied my name.—Revelations 3:8

S tay the course. If the situation bends you, just know the promises of God are always there to protect and comfort you. Continue to give your all to the commandments of the Lord, and He will fulfill His plans for your life. He knows the thoughts He has toward us. Man can't put us where God wants us to go.

I was assigned the duty of monitoring the playground of an elementary school during four recess periods each day. Physically, no one knew how I felt other than the two ladies that accompanied me each day for playground duty. We prepared with all the warm gear that we could put on for the wintery days. Through the hot and cold days, we were there building relationships with the students and each other. I know God had me there to protect and pray for students. It was doing those days that the Lord said, "I am the only one that can take you from the playground to another position."

It was during the playground experience that God assured me that He is always there. I was nearing the end of a week-long fast when a third grade student approached me and asked if I was a Christian. Of course I answered yes. His next comment was, "I knew it, because you have the Christian glow." I knew that God had sent a little boy to encourage me and that there is more activity on the playground taking place than what is seen with the natural eye.

Over the course of time, I applied for other positions. The message from God was simply to wait on Him. The confirmation to wait came from an individual that stated, "The Lord said delayed, but not denied." The next position came with the self-imposed playground duty to continue what God started. I knew I must continue to watch and pray for students on the playground. Remember to wait on the Lord and He will give you the desires of your heart.

My Prayer:

_____

_____

_____

_____

_____

His Voice:

_____

_____

_____

_____

_____

My Action:

_____

_____

_____

_____

_____

Day 7

Escape

I will go before thee, and make the crooked places straight: I will break in pieces the gates of brass, and cut in sunder the bars of iron.—Isaiah 45:2

We can't fight against the enemy without God on our side. He protects and gives us a plan to overcome all of the obstacles in our lives. The power of God is ever present if we follow His voice and listen to His Word.

As I sat down to write about surrendering to the Lord, He showed me how He is in the midst of all that we do when we are centered on Him. I was researching information on the phrase "Balm in Gilead." The television was blasting in the other room. All I could hear was random profanity. My thought was, "Lord, how can I do this?" I did not want to ask that the channel be changed. Each moment I could feel the distraction was becoming more intense. As I continued to talk to God, I asked, "How can I concentrate on your message and desires for me?" I printed the words of the song "There is a Balm in Gilead" from the Internet. As the printed paper lay on the printer, I continued to look up scriptures about the balm. In the midst of the background noise out rang the song I had just printed from the television. God gave me a sense of calm and humored me, too. This was God's way of telling me when we try to figure it out, He already has it worked out. It is true. If we make one step toward Him, He will make two toward us and make our crooked places straight.

There are so many "but God" things that happen that let us know that God is the one and only God. He is ever present and ready to intervene for us. "Ah Lord GOD! Behold, thou hast made the heaven and the earth by thy great power and stretched out thine arm, and there is nothing too hard for thee" (Jeremiah 32:17).

My Prayer:

_____

_____

_____

_____

_____

His Voice:

_____

_____

_____

_____

_____

My Action:

_____

_____

_____

_____

_____

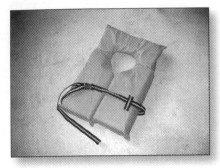

Fear of Drowning

Fear thou not; for I am with thee; be not dismayed; for I am thy God: I will strengthen thee; yea, I will help thee; yea, I will uphold thee with the right hand of my righteousness.—Isaiah 41:10

Fear prevents us from being successful. Fear of failure translates into fear of the unknown in relationships, jobs, projects, and business transactions. Fear keeps our dreams hostage and keeps us in a stalemate position. There is no failure in God. He promises to sustain every believer. Yet we procrastinate and hesitate to step into the water. As believers, Christ Jesus is our Savior and a life preserver that guides us and protects us from drowning.

While vacationing with my husband for our twentieth wedding anniversary, we decided to go to a beautiful small, clear white sandy beach to snorkel. My swimming skills can't be compared to my husband's. I knew my limitations, so I dared not venture too far out. However, I began enjoying the beauty of the water and all that it yielded underneath. Huge rocks protruded from the depths of the water. I saw my husband sitting on a big rock and decided that I would swim to him. Before I could reach him, I thought that I would stand up. But when I stood up, I didn't feel the bottom. Of course, I panicked. My fear of drowning was staring me in the face. My husband realized my distress and swam to me and said, "Just calm down and swim. You can swim; if you don't, you will make me drown, too." Spiritually, God is telling us not to panic, but instead to step off the shore and into the water. He will be there with His hands to guide us each and every step of the way.

Listen as God asks, "What would you do if …?" Make a list of those things. What could we accomplish if we knew that we would be successful? Let's step out on faith with our list. What is stopping us from being and doing the things that are written down? Is it that we have not put legs on our dreams and goals? God tells us each day in His Word: "All things are possible through Christ Jesus." Remember that the things that are listed are just little things according to God. "God is able to do exceedingly abundantly above what we can ever imagine" (Ephesians 3:20). So it's not God that is hesitating. If God tells us to do something, what is preventing us from doing His work, other than ourselves? God will help us through the rough spots.

My Prayer:

_____

_____

_____

_____

_____

His Voice:

_____

_____

_____

_____

My Action:

_____

_____

_____

_____

_____

Day 9

Give Thanks

He that planted the ear, shall he not hear? He that formed the eye, shall he not see?—Psalms 94:9

It took me a while to understand the phrase, "In all things give thanks." It just didn't seem right. How could I say, "Oh, thank you, Lord, for all the things that cause headaches and heartaches." It was through the many tears that I realized that by giving God praises, everything becomes alright. It's an awesome feeling to know that whatever goes on in your life, you can go to God and He will make it all right. Now, I know that there is nothing too hard for God. Our existence is a thing of the past. God has already determined our future.

When we realize that we are on life's stage, we are able to accept our roles of becoming the best "characters" that God sees as He looks from the balcony (heaven) onto the stage (earth). Then possibilities and promises will start to flow into our lives. Each day we must be the best characters. We must continually practice to be Christlike in everything we say and do. God hears our every prayer and sees our every action. As you start a new day, remember that the battles of the mind are to cause weakness, stress, and defeat, which cause us to miss our cues. Pray to respond to every situation with Godly wisdom and act in ways that are pleasing in His sight. Continue to seek higher ground and a greater anointing in the Lord. Prayer and praise are truly the most important things in life.

My Prayer:

_____

_____

_____

_____

_____

His Voice:

_____

_____

_____

_____

_____

My Action:

_____

_____

_____

_____

_____

Go Deep!

Now when He had left speaking, He said unto Simon, Launch out into the deep, and let down your nets for a draught.—Luke 5:4

When Simon was finished for the day and felt he had done all that he could do and had given up, Jesus stepped onto the ship. He continued to teach from the ship, prayed for Simon, and gave him instructions to go further into the water. Even though Simon knew in his heart he had worked all night with no results, he was obedient. Simon and his crew were probably tired and despondent. But when Simon acted upon God's words by going deeper and lowering his net, he received an abundance of fish. The reward of obedience exceeded Simon's expectations; it raised him higher in the Lord eyes. He fell on his knees in repentance and awe. The amount of fish available became so many that he didn't have room to receive them all and needed to call for additional help (see Luke 5:1–8).

God wants us to go deeper in our Christian walk and talk. It is time for us to stop being surface worshippers. We must increase our faith and dig deeper to gain the fullness of Christ Jesus. Going deep is to have undeniable faith in the promises of God. He can do all things and everything but fail. Just when we think we are walking and talking according to His Word, the Lord calls us higher by saying, "Go deeper." Miracles are being performed every day and God promises greater miracles to come. What is so special about God is that He sent His son Jesus and His Holy Spirit to accompany us every step of the way. Our journey of going deeper for the Master comes with the assurance that He is always by our sides.

Our charge is to hold on, have faith, and seek to bring others into the knowledge of Christ. The presence of the Lord is constant in every situation in our lives. Whatever we are going through, we must not give up, give in, or run away. Keep the faith by going deeper into His Word so that God can bring you up higher.

My Prayer:

_____

_____

_____

_____

_____

His Voice:

_____

_____

_____

_____

_____

My Action:

_____

_____

_____

_____

_____

Go Fish!

Notwithstanding, lest we should offend them, go thou to the sea, and cast a hook, and take up the fish that first cometh up; and when thou hast opened his mouth, thou shalt find a piece of money; that take, and give unto them for me and thee.—Matthew 17:27

The card game Go Fish is an old favorite that is enjoyed by all ages. However, when God tells us to "go fish," the rules are not the same as in the card game. God doesn't want us to pass up or discard individuals. He simply wants us to be fishers of men. Being obedient to God's Word is one of His ways of providing for us. The voice of the Lord guiding us may cause many to ponder instead of take action. When we follow the path of righteousness, the Lord will make a way for us. Jesus knows the demands that are placed upon those who are called by His name—His chosen.

In Capernaum, Jesus vowed to keep peace with all men. In order to shut the mouths of the tax collectors, He opened the mouth of the fish and instructed Peter to take the first fish out of the sea and there would be enough money to pay the taxes for Peter and Him. There wouldn't be a need to pull from the sea again. He said, "The first fish that comes up would supply all their needs and the needs of others" (see Matthew 17:27). Spiritually, we must read the Word to find the promises of God and store them in our hearts. His words are enough to feed us and others.

Many that find themselves in a tough place wonder what they should change to bring God's favor into their lives. Mainly, it is discovering the will of God, which is His Word. We are carrying a bait and hook provided by God to prosper us, which is our purpose for being on earth. When we are faced with heartaches and hardships, we are instructed to cast our burdens and all of our cares upon Him and He will give us rest (see Psalms 55:22). My pastor says repeatedly to the congregation, "It just doesn't make sense to pray and worry." God doesn't want us to worry or have any anxiety in our lives. Practice and discipline is needed to build a close relationship with God. Things that we tend to worry about have already been taken care by God (see Luke 12:22–25). It doesn't matter how much we think about a situation; it will not change until God intervenes. It is through Christ Jesus that our blessings flow. He wants us to depend totally upon Him.

When God says, "Go fish," He is asking us to be diligent in our hunger and thirst for His Word, to bring others into the knowledge of Christ, and to trust Him to supply all of our needs "according to His riches and glory" (see Philippians 4:19). Lord, what must I do to further your work? When you focus on doing the work of the Lord, He will provide for your every need and the needs of others.

My Prayer:

_____

_____

_____

_____

_____

His Voice:

_____

_____

_____

_____

My Action:

_____

_____

_____

_____

God Specializes

And Jesus said unto them, Because of your unbelief: for verily I say unto you, If ye have faith as a grain of mustard seed, ye shall say unto this mountain, Remove hence to yonder place; and it shall remove; and nothing shall be impossible unto you.—Matthew 17:20

What's your specialty? It may be making the best home-cooked dish, being crafty, public speaking, crunching numbers, or doing yard work. The list can go on and on. *Webster's Dictionary* defines specialize as follows: "As to apply or direct to a particular end, use, or to concentrate one's efforts in a special activity, or field." Sometimes we have problems that seem impossible to solve.

Our quest to gain assistance for a specific need is unyielding; we find ways or someone to take care of the situation. Hopefully, the best expert or top specialist has been recommended. We accept referrals to individuals that specialize in the area of concern. Sometimes, after spending countless hours researching the cause of the problem being diagnosed, it defies and bewilders everyone that the problem or cause is undetectable. We must keep in mind that people "practice" all things while God "perfects" all things. The answer to all of our problems lies at the feet of Jesus.

The cause and the cure are in the Master's hands. He specializes in things impossible. God wants us to believe in Him, acknowledge His Son Jesus Christ, His words, and have a little faith that He will do just what He said He would do. God only asks for a little faith, the size of a mustard seed (see Matthew 17:20). The beauty of knowing God is that you can go to your omnipotent, omnipresent specialist to meet your individual needs.

My Prayer:

_____

_____

_____

_____

_____

His Voice:

_____

_____

_____

_____

_____

My Action:

_____

_____

_____

_____

_____

Here I Am, Lord ... Send Me!

Also, I heard the voice of the Lord saying, Whom shall I send, and who will go for us? Then said I, Here am I; send me.
—Isaiah 6:8

We must let the Lord know through our relationship with Him, our words, and our actions that we are ready to say, "Here I am Lord to do your will and carry your Word." God is looking for travel agents to be ready and willing to do His work in the land that He created. God gives us jobs to do for Him. Being willing to be used by God is a total surrender of our biases and fears. Surrendering is following Jesus without hesitation. The first words from the song, *Where He Lead Me* says, "Where He leads me I will follow; I will go with Him all the way." Truly you can expect to be used by God in a special way. We may not know where we are asking God to send us. Just saying, "I will go, do, and be," will allow you to be a part of the Master's plan for your life.

In April 2007, near the end of the school year, I went through the long process of applying for a new position. In addition to two interviews before a panel, another criterion for the position was to complete a performance event to demonstrate knowledge, research, and technology skills. I remember standing in the congregation one Sunday during morning worship praying and praising God when the Lord spoke to me and said, "Be ready." Without hesitation, I went back to work the next day and started packing my office. As I waited on the confirmation week after week, I continued to pack and clean out files. When the official call came offering the position, I was packed and ready to go. Following God's wisdom and direction, I was prepared for the quick transition to the new position. Spiritually, that is the readiness God wants from us. Ask Him, "What is the work that You would have me to do?" Be spiritually and physically ready to go when He calls.

A dear church mother and friend would often tell me that she was "packing heavy." Packing heavy means she had been before the Lord in prayer and scripture. She was ready to go forth and provide others with the inspired words that God had given to her in her continuous devotion to Him. Sometimes she would say, "This is straight off the press." We must be ready to speak God's Word and to be used by Him. God wants us ready in season and out of season, when we feel like it or not. Be ready, packed in the anointing of the Holy Spirit, so that when God is looking for someone to send on mission work, you are in a position to say, "Here I am Lord … send me!"

My Prayer:

_____

_____

_____

_____

_____

His Voice:

_____

_____

_____

_____

_____

My Action:

_____

_____

_____

_____

_____

Day 14

I Was There

Humble yourselves in the sight of the Lord, and he will lift you up.—James 4:10

Can you see and experience God's glory from where you are spiritually? If the answer is no, then you must change your perspective. Often we look at positions of authority and power and allow that to become a status symbol. We must humble ourselves before God, for He has promised to lift us up.

During morning devotion, I began to thank God for pouring His spirit upon me during a church conference I attended earlier in the week. Why was that service so fulfilling and different from other church services I had attended? Could it be because I went with a specific and urgent need to be filled and an unstoppable spirit of expectation to receive a spiritual blessing from the Lord? My need was so deep that I arrived thirty minutes early and positioned myself on the front row. I sought front row seating to receive a fresh anointing. I simply wanted to be drenched with a Word from the Lord. That night, I received a Word and a blessing from the Lord. Every word spoken was meat for my starving soul. As I continued to thank God for His restorative power, the Lord said to me, "I was there."

God doesn't look at titles or positions; He focuses on the heart, mind, and soul. When we humble ourselves before the Lord, there is no situation or circumstance that He will not bring us through. God showers us with an outpouring of His Holy Spirit to let us know He is with us always.

My Prayer:

_____

_____

_____

_____

_____

His Voice:

_____

_____

_____

_____

_____

My Action:

_____

_____

_____

_____

_____

In the Name of *Jesus*!

*By stretching forth thine hand to heal;
and that signs and wonders may be done
by the name of thy holy child Jesus.—*
Acts 4:30

When we wake up each morning, our minds immediately focus on the demands of the day. Sometimes there is so much on our minds to be accomplished, especially during customary celebratory events and special holidays. It hardly seems possible to accomplish each task and be there for everyone and everything. When you are feeling overwhelmed and everything is happening at once, focus on the word of the day—Jesus.

There is so much power in the name of Jesus. Think about the bracelets, plaques, and novelties that have the inscription, "What Would Jesus Do?" It's not what He would do that we should ask ourselves. We should practice praying and saying, "In the name of Jesus." Command that the situation or circumstance change by focusing and calling on the name of Jesus. What does Jesus supply to His believers through the use of His name?

Knowing the life, death, and resurrection of Jesus, we know that the name Jesus is so much more than just a name. In Jesus' name there is healing for pain, blessings, and deliverance for sacrifice, peace, and freedom for distress, victory for test and trials, and joy for strength. It's all in His name. Call on the name of Jesus and be blessed beyond measure. God has given us authority and spiritual power to use Jesus' name in prayer for deliverance in every situations, which sends the devil packing. Using the name of Jesus is the key to binding the evil spirit and losing the Holy Spirit for things in heaven and on earth. Jesus said: "Whatever ye shall ask the father in my name, he will give it to you" (John 16:23).

My Prayer:

_____

_____

_____

_____

_____

His Voice:

_____

_____

_____

_____

_____

My Action:

_____

_____

_____

_____

_____

It's Time to Shout!

*And it came to pass at the seventh time, when the priests blew with the trumpets, Joshua said unto the people, Shout; for the LORD hath given you the city.—*Joshua 6:16.

Faith in God doesn't allow us to remain captives outside the walls of prosperity. As we walk through our daily lives, we allow the enemy of circumstances to prevent us from feeling and experiencing the joy of the Lord. By obtaining the "Now faith" that is mentioned in Hebrews 11:1, we have the assurance and hope of those things that are not seen. I am sure that when Joshua gave instructions to the people of Israel to march around the wall for six days and then seven times on the seventh day, they realized the impact of crying out in a loud voice. Through their obedience and loud cries, the wall of Jericho came down and they were able to take the city.

It is time for us to shout out loud and destroy the things that have caused a wall to come between us and living an abundant life through Christ Jesus. Shout out loud to destroy and tear down the walls of despair, depression, self-doubt, disease, deceit, defeat, and demonic forces. Shouting to the Lord gets His attention, the attention of others, and puts the enemy on the run. It also motivates, excites, and energizes us to do what God has always wanted us to do for Him. We become inspired through our praise and prayer life. You have what you need within you to become greater than you are today. Gain access to victory by shouting, for the Lord has given us the city.

My Prayer:

_____

_____

_____

_____

_____

His Voice:

_____

_____

_____

_____

_____

My Action:

_____

_____

_____

_____

_____

Lead Me

From the end of the earth will I cry unto thee, when my heart is overwhelmed: lead me to the rock that is higher than I.—Psalms 61:2

Following directions and being guided automatically makes us followers. God wants us to be doers and followers of His Word. We start out on a path and find ourselves wondering, *Should I stay on this track, or should I jump ship?* We have so many uncertainties when trying to plot our own courses. Remember God's words come to guide us every step of the way.

When I find myself in a situation of uncertainty, I ask God to enter into the room before me. I realize there is no need to second-guess myself or question what I will do or how I will get there. Whenever I walk into a room for a presentation, interview, or meeting, I say, "Lord, you go in the door first." I will literally step back in a subtle pause to privately acknowledge that God's presence has to be with me. Where I am there He promised to be also, "Even there shall thy hand lead me, and thy right hand shall hold me" (Psalms 139:1).

Ask God to order your steps and guide you through life's journeys. Let Him know that you want to be led by Him. Followers of Christ are led by the Master leader. In Isaiah 42:16, the Master leader gives us assurances to comfort us by saying, "He brings the blind by a way *that* they knew not; I will lead them in paths *that* they have not known: I will make darkness light before them, and crooked things straight. These things will I do unto them, and not forsake them."

We don't know the destinations that God has predestined for us. When we ask God to lead us, it is a faith walk. To step out on His promises is to allow God to direct your path and to be led by Him.

My Prayer:

_____

_____

_____

_____

_____

His Voice:

_____

_____

_____

_____

_____

My Action:

_____

_____

_____

_____

_____

Let it Snow

Not that I speak in respect of want: for I have learned, in whatsoever state I am, therewith to be content.—Philippians 4:11

M any people become apprehensive and feel stuck or trapped when it snows. For most, snow is an immobilizer, but I worked with an exceptionally energetic woman who would get so excited about the sight of snow that she made others joyful. Everyone would watch her childlike glee and smile. I don't think that it was that she wanted the day off or thought about the difficulty of driving or cleaning the driveway. She simply enjoyed the beauty of the element that God created.

Without a doubt, snow is cold, wet, and potentially dangerous if we are not careful. However, seeing the glass as half full rather than half empty is the key to receiving the reward of the snow day. Naturally, when it snows we automatically think that productivity decreases. Schools and businesses may close and scheduled activities and meetings are often cancelled. What we thought we had control of is suddenly out of our hands.

I admit, I think everything in my life happens for my good, just because I love God. Sure, I have projects from work that I purposefully bring home if snow is expected and housework that I focus on during the shut in. But I realize the real reason that I am stuck at home is so God can refocus me on Him. All the work that I do for my secular job cannot compare to the work that I do for God's glory. This is also a time that God gives His people to enter into His rest. Resting in the Lord relaxes us from the constant day to day items that keep us busy each moment of the day. If you are in a relationship with God, He is jealous and wants to spend time with you. During the day(s) of rest, God shows us that there is calm, comfort, and peace given to our circumstances wherever He dwells. Spend unexpected days away from the routine of the work day to focus on God by glorifying, praying, and reading the Word.

My Prayer:

_____

_____

_____

_____

_____

His Voice:

_____

_____

_____

_____

_____

My Action:

_____

_____

_____

_____

_____

Life is a Vapor

Whereas ye know not what shall be on the morrow. For what is your life? It is even a vapour that appeareth for a little time, and then vanisheth away.—James 4:14

Each moment of breath that we experience is a blessing from God. So many times we take for granted that our next breath will automatically come to us effortlessly and without thought. Early one Sunday morning as I prepared for church, I received an emergency call about a student who had had several heart transplants that caused me to make a detour. Upon entering the family waiting room for the former student, I was informed that the doctors had given up. His third heart transplant was failing. The Lord led me to his bedside, away from his family and friends that had gathered in prayer. As I walked closer to the student's hospital bed I watched his frail body struggle deeply for each breath. I remember saying, "Lord, you know him from the crown of his head to the soles of his feet."

There I realized that life is a vapor. We are visible as living human beings and invisible through death. At any moment our circumstances and situation can change. Are we ready for the change from mortality to immortality? Life is uncertain, but death is sure. The Word of God tells us that "no man knows the time or the hour when the Lord will come." We must spiritually connect with the glory of God's magnificent gift to breathe. Try to fully see the beauty of life in all of your experiences. Living each day to the fullest doesn't mean living life your way, but God's way. His way is outlined in the Ten Commandments (see Exodus 20). When you obey His commandments, He knows you value His sacrifice and gift of everlasting life.

As a little girl growing up in Memphis, I remember frequent trips to small rural towns in Arkansas with my parents to visit my grandparents and great-grandparents. Many times my brothers, sisters, and I would just sit as my parents checked on elderly relatives. Now I know that those visits were just precious vapors to connect us with family.

Life is a vapor and our charge is to reach out and touch the lives of others as we pass through. It may mean making an effort to connect with family, friends, and individuals who cross our paths. It may mean sharing words of encouragement. Your presence just might breathe life into the lives others, to give them hope and the will to continue their journeys. Years have passed; the dying boy lived and is now man. He and his family are very much a part of my life, thoughts, and prayers. He is a high school student receiving the love and support of his caring family and many others. Let's breathe hope into the lives of others. Life is a vapor.

My Prayer:

_____

_____

_____

_____

_____

His Voice:

_____

_____

_____

_____

_____

My Action:

_____

_____

_____

_____

_____

Day 20

Make a List

Ask, and it shall be given you; seek, and ye shall find; knock, and the door shall be open unto you.—Matthew 7:7

Have you ever received a list of wishes from someone for Christmas or a birthday? Or maybe you've observed the person enough to know what he desires or needs. In the spirit of the holiday season, we strive to give gifts to our family, friends, and coworkers. We beat ourselves up mentally and financially trying to be there for everyone during this time of year, even to the point of saying, "It is better to give than to receive," and we go into credit card debt that often lasts a year or more. It doesn't matter how many lists you are carrying around as you do your holiday shopping; the most important list must be intentionally created by you.

Solomon knew what was at the top of his list when he was asked by the Father. One night God appeared to Solomon and said, "Ask for whatever you want me to give you."

Solomon answered, "You have shown great kindness to David my father and have made me king in his place. Now, LORD God, let your promise to my father David be confirmed, for you have made me king over a people who are as numerous as the dust of the earth. Give me wisdom and knowledge, that I may lead this people, for who is able to govern this great people of yours?"

God replied, "Since this is your heart's desire and you have not asked for wealth, riches or honor, nor for the death of your enemies, and since you have not asked for a long life but for wisdom and knowledge to govern my people over whom I have made you king, therefore wisdom and knowledge will be given you. And I will also give you wealth, riches and honor, such as no king who was before you ever had and none after you will have" (see 2 Chronicles 1:7–12).

Imagine hearing a child say to his or her father, "Here's my Christmas list." Everyday our Father is waiting for a list from His children. We should prayerfully make a list of things that we desire from God. My first list was on a small yellow pad. I carried the list for many years; it became tattered from being carried in my wallet. As I prayed for the list and God blessed, I would date the items on the list and continue to pray that His will be done in my life. Every time I looked at the list of God's blessings and the dates, which were sometimes close together and sometimes far apart, I would become full with His awesomeness just thinking about what only my heavenly Father provides for those who love Him. Since that first list, I have had to start on another list. My first list became a talking point. I wanted everyone to know the power of God, to believe and have faith in His promises. The list was my proof that God is who He says He is. Make a list of things that you want from God. Watch and pray for miracles to take place in your life and the lives of others.

My Prayer:

_____

_____

_____

_____

_____

His Voice:

_____

_____

_____

_____

_____

My Action:

_____

_____

_____

_____

_____

My List

Delight thyself also in the Lord; and he shall give thee the desires of thine heart. Commit thy way unto the Lord; trust also in him; and he shall bring it to pass. Psalms 37: 4-5 If ye abide in me, and my words abide in you, ye shall ask what ye will, and it shall be done unto you. John 15:7.

My Desire: _____

_____

_____

_____

_____

Date Granted: _____

My Desire: _____

_____

_____

_____

_____

Date Granted: _____

My Desire: _____

_____

_____

_____

_____

Date Granted: _____

Now, Unto Him

Now unto Him that is able to keep you from falling, and to present you faultless before the presence of His glory with exceeding joy.—Jude 1:24

God has given us access to everything through His son, Christ Jesus. It started with the first six days when He formed the world. God placed man and woman in the Garden of Eden, or what some may call paradise on earth, to live forever. It is because of man's disobedience that He gave us His son Jesus to die for our sins. He tells us that He would be with us even until the end of the world. Now it is up to us to live the life that God has placed at our feet. Can we pick up the life that God has given to us and put total trust in Him by giving God glory? God is able to keep us from falling. It is now up to us serve Him. He has proven His selfless love toward us repeatedly. Now can we say unto you Lord, I give my life, to serve, trust, and live for your glory?

All of the provisions for an abundant life have been made through Christ Jesus. God is more than able to keep us from falling. What makes us afraid to step out of our comfort zone and pursue those things that are already planned for our lives? God can keep us from falling naturally and spiritually. "For I know the thoughts that I think toward you, saith the Lord, thoughts of peace, and not of evil, to give you an expected end" (Jeremiah 29:11).

God has completed the individualized plans for our lives. It is now up to us to fulfill those plans through the promises that have already been made. It is up to us to live in such as way that will make God's plans a reality in our lives. He knows His thoughts toward us. He wants to bring us to an expected end—which is peace and prosperity through His promises. Know that your blessings are signed, sealed, and waiting for delivery. Blessings are evoked though prayer and praise. "Seek ye first the kingdom of God, and His righteousness; and all these things shall be added unto you" (Matthew 6:33).

My Prayer:

_____

_____

_____

_____

_____

His Voice:

_____

_____

_____

_____

_____

My Action:

_____

_____

_____

_____

_____

Our Daily Bread

Our Father which art in heaven, Hallowed be thy name. Thy kingdom come. Thy will be done in earth, as it is in heaven. Give us this day our daily bread. And forgive us our debts, as we forgive our debtors. And lead us not into temptation, but deliver us from evil: For thine is the kingdom, and the power, and the glory, for ever. Amen.— Matthew 6:9–13

Even though the Christmas season rapidly passes and all the festivities end as a new year begins, hope remains for the year ahead. Joyfulness and thankfulness abound for what's ahead. Live each day with great expectations for miracles. Always look to hear from the Lord and have Him manifest Himself in your life. Matthew 6:9–13 is a familiar prayer that many feel they have outgrown, but there is so much more to this "little big" prayer. One year during the holiday season, I could not shake the phrase, "Give us this day our daily bread." God's Word brings daily messages to bless our souls. God feeds us our daily meals. Open your ears to hear and receive your blessings by giving God glory for the things He has done and will do for you through reading His Word each day, which is your daily bread.

It was Christmas 1999, and my two sisters and their four children spent the holiday with my family. Before they left, they went shopping and returned with a collectible 1999 Cloisonné ornament. The ornaments range between twenty and forty-five dollars each. They are handmade in Beijing, China, from fine copper wire in filigree patterns and enamel filling, firing, and polishing with brilliant colors and great artistic designs. Since then, I made it a practice to purchase personalized name ornaments at after-Christmas sales to give coworkers and friends the following year. One year, as I picked out ornaments for my coworkers, the Lord whispered, "You will not be there next year." So I put the ornaments down and went to the Christmas cards, selected some of the cards that were marked 50 percent off, but then put them down, too. I left the after-Christmas sale empty-handed.

During the course of the morning, I proceeded to another store across town to look for January birthday gifts. My husband, daughter, and one of my sons share the same week. I was able to purchase two sixty-dollar sweaters for a total of twenty-seven dollars for my husband. Thank you, Lord was my song of praise, for I knew that was a true blessing. I went on to another after-Christmas sale and saw a pewter platter that read, "Our Daily Bread." I wanted that platter so badly; it just touched my spirit. What could be better than to have the platter as a constant reminder on my kitchen counter? Once again, I thought, I don't have money for this, but I really like it. I left the store without the platter. My next destination was to make it to the store to purchase the annual Cloisonné ornament. I returned home with my sweaters and an ornament that was a replica of Noah's Ark.

During the following week, I happened to be in a Christian bookstore and saw the same pewter platter there. Everywhere I turned, there was this platter saying, "Our Daily Bread." However, I resisted getting it again. On the following Saturday, my husband and I invited several couples over to fellowship with us to celebrate the Christmas season. At the end of the evening, as my husband and I were cleaning up and putting things away, with a quick glance I noticed a gift under the tree. I asked my husband, "What was it?" He said, "One of the couples brought the gift." Very tired and ready for bed, I grabbed the present without much thought and unwrapped it to find the platter that read, "Our Daily Bread." Needless to say, my tiredness was replaced with renewed strength and joy from above.

Just as God had whispered during my shopping trip, I did receive a promotion that following year. God elevated me to a new position. If God told Noah what actions to take in building the ark, He will do the same today for us. There is a plan and a purpose for our lives. Ask for your daily bread and receive the spiritual nourishment that will sustain you through your days, weeks, months, and years.

My Prayer:

_____

_____

_____

_____

_____

His Voice:

_____

_____

_____

_____

_____

My Action:

_____

_____

_____

_____

_____

Day 23

Passionate Prayers

O Lord, hear; O Lord, forgive; O Lord, hearken and do; defer not, for thine own sake, O my God: for thy city and thy people are called by thy name.—Daniel 9:19

The passion of Daniel's prayer for the Jews and Jerusalem is felt in each word written in Daniel 9:19. When we are asked to speak or write for an audience, we make numerous edits or revisions before we are pleased with a final copy to present. There was no need for Daniel to go through the editing process. He went before God without hesitation and spoke with passionate, precise, and faith-filled words that caused God to raise an eyebrow and move on behalf of the people who, as Daniel respectfully said, are called by God's name (Daniel 9:19). This touched the heart of God. Daniel was saying, "Lord, the people belong to you. Do something now, defer not!" God takes delight in hearing the Word. Praying the Word yields results.

Today as never before, we must pray as Daniel prayed, with passion and intense emotions for God to intervene on behalf of His people. We must edit out the filler words and speak specifically and directly to God in our prayers. Using unnecessary words is considered babbling and vain repetition (see Matthew 6:7). Daniel was concise and didn't beat around the bush. He physically put himself in the prayer to intercede on behalf of others.

Similar to Daniel's prayer is the prayer of Jabez: "And Jabez called on the God of Israel, saying, 'Oh that thou wouldest bless me indeed, and enlarge my coast, and that thine hand might be with me, and that thou wouldest keep [me] from evil, that it may not grieve me!'" (see, 1 Chronicles 4:10). Both prayers are short but mighty in the sight of God. As Jabez and Daniel did, you must first live a life that pleases the Father, so when you go to Him in prayer, you will have His ear. He listens to His children and supplies their needs according to His riches and glory—as promised (see Philippians 4:19). O Lord, help me to hear and act on your word!

My Prayer:

_____

_____

_____

_____

_____

His Voice:

_____

_____

_____

_____

_____

My Action:

_____

_____

_____

_____

_____

Peace

Peace I leave with you, my peace I give unto you, not as the world giveth, give I unto you; Let not your heart be troubled, neither let it be afraid.—John 14:27

The world's understanding of peace is very different from the spiritual meaning of peace. Peace is more than a mere symbol. The world only touches the surface of the true meaning of peace. *Merriam Webster's Dictionary* defines peace as follows: a state of tranquility or quiet and freedom from disquieting or oppressive thoughts or emotions and harmony in personal relations.

God wants us to be in perfect peace with ourselves and others. Our instructions are to hold our peace and let the Lord fight our battles. We can go through the practice of outwardly wearing the symbol for peace and making the hand gesture for peace, but inner peace comes only from above. Nothing compares to having the peace of God in our hearts, which is the third fruit of the Spirit (see Galatians 5:22–23). When we have spiritual peace, others notice the inexplicable calm, strength, and contentedness in our demeanors.

Jesus exercised great peace when He carried His cross and died for our sins. In my mind, that exemplified true peace that surpassed all understanding. We must seek peace in all things (mind, body, health, finance, etc.). When we are quiet, we win the battle over inner anguish, worry, and turmoil. Our minds are no longer disturbed. There is peace in the midst of our personal and public storms. Peace will abide in our homes, workplaces, and in our relationships with others. Our charge is to hold our peace and let the Lord fight our battles. When you don't have the peace of God in your heart, there resides the enemy and you sin against God's authority to provide you with the peace that your Comforter gives—the peace that surpass all understanding.

My Prayer:

_____

_____

_____

_____

_____

His Voice:

_____

_____

_____

_____

_____

My Action:

_____

_____

_____

_____

_____

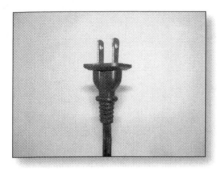

Power

Now unto Him that is able to do exceeding abundantly above all that we ask or think, according to the power that worketh in us.—Ephesians 3:20

In Ephesians 3:11–21, authority is given through the Holy Ghost to exercise and experience the magnitude of God's glory. We have the power to change our circumstances. Positional power allows us to move the tangible, whereas spiritual power allows us to move the intangible. God gives us power to move the mountains in our lives. Holy Ghost power is real God-given power. God showers us with more spiritual strength to carry on and fight the battles that are before us. When we don't exercise our God-given power, we don't realize the breadth, length, depth, or height of the power that already resides within us to effect change in our lives and the lives of others. Exercise your power today to encourage and motivate others to experience the love of God.

One of my sons shared with me a message he received during a college campus Bible study session. The speaker simply said, "When we lift our hands in praise, we are plugging into the power of God." The message is to stay plugged into the power source. Praying, reading the Word, and giving God praise are ways to maintain our spiritual strength or power. During natural power outages, our spiritual source of power can remain strong if we continue to seek His will in our lives.

While standing outdoors, I looked upward and marveled at the many poles carrying uniformed swaying electrical lines. These electrical connections, which exist on the outside, allow many businesses to operate on the inside. That is exactly what God wants. If we take His Word to heart, His power will show on the outside. Moments later, a car passed me with a magnetic business advertisement on the side that read, "Power." I am not sure what type of business it was, but for me the spiritual connection was to get more Holy Ghost power by staying connected to God's Word.

My Prayer:

_____

_____

_____

_____

_____

His Voice:

_____

_____

_____

_____

_____

My Action:

_____

_____

_____

_____

_____

Day 26

Praise Him

I WILL bless the Lord at all times: his praise shall continually be in my mouth.—Psalms 34:1

Every day is a gift from the Lord. "This is the day that the Lord has made; I will rejoice and be glad!" During the course of a day, we may be faced with many encounters. Many situations come in the form of a test, trial, or tribulation that we must pass. Some jobs require testing prior to employment to obtain licensure and certification. I have paid to attend study sessions and take several costly exams.

During one of the testing sessions, a friend and I decided to go to the ladies room to pray before entering the testing room. Immediately after the test I began to think about how I should have answered things differently. But God would not let me stay in that state of thinking too long. He made me realize that it was His test, not mine. I did not understand it until He spoke to me in the shower during my waiting period for the results.

God said, "How would you praise me if …?"

I said, "What?"

He softly said again, "How you would praise me if …, and I realized he wanted me to fill in the blank. Oh, my God—I praised God in the shower that day. I filled in so many needs, wants, and desires. My tears of praise mixed with the natural water. I praised God from that day forward for passing the exam.

When the results came in the mail, I continued to praise God while opening the letter. I ran down the driveway praising God. For the first time I was able to walk in my house and scream at the top of my lungs, "Thank you, Jesus!" I had never screamed "thank you" to Jesus in the house before. My scores were above the state average. There is truly nothing too hard for God to accomplish if you believe. Give God a "What if…" praise.

My Prayer:

_____

_____

_____

_____

_____

His Voice:

_____

_____

_____

_____

_____

My Action:

_____

_____

_____

_____

_____

Day 27

Purified for Service

And He shall sit as a refiner and purifier of silver; and He shall purify the sons of Levi, and purge them as gold and silver, that they may offer unto the Lord an offering in righteousness.—Malachi 3:3

When test and trials come to true seekers of God, we must know that He is only purifying us for His service. There is great joy and peace in the purification process. Like Job, we must stand firm and say with all our might, "Though the enemy slay me, yet will I trust in God." Thinking about all the things that Job went through, we must ask God for the strength of Job when our tests come. How willing are you to be used by God for His service?

When we go to church, we tend to rate the service and the speaker. We should rate our own service to God. Ask Him daily to purify your body and soul for His service and to be blessed with His presence. "Every man that hath this hope in Him purifieth himself, even as He is pure" (1 John 3:3). Getting ready to serve God requires a garment of praise and a robe of righteousness. There is no way that we can be used for God's service until we present ourselves as living sacrifices, holy, acceptable unto God, which is our reasonable service (Romans 12:1). We must serve as a vessel for God and work toward being clean and without blemish. Asking to be purified is asking for the heat to be turned up in our lives. We must stand the heat to pass the test. Look at the endurance of Jesus Christ for our sins. He was already pure, but he died for our purity.

Purifying our heart for God's service requires action. Ask for forgiveness from sin in your life and forgive those that you feel have caused you harm. Jesus' simple prayer said, "Forgive us our debts, as we forgive our debtors (Matthew 6:12). When you purify yourself, you remove sin and guilt that you cause and allow others to place upon you. Purification increases your concentration and focus on God. We are promised that the pure in heart shall see God.

My Prayer:

_____

_____

_____

_____

_____

His Voice:

_____

_____

_____

_____

_____

My Action:

_____

_____

_____

_____

_____

Road Trip

Make a joyful noise unto the Lord, all ye lands. Serve the Lord with gladness: come before His presence with singing.
—Psalms 100:1–2

Traveling is just one of the things in life that can take you places. My preferred mode of transportation is the airplane. However, for short trips, I find myself looking forward to being in my car. I give God glory for my ability to travel on paved roads and bridges to just about every place imaginable.

Each time we make plans to travel, the road before us takes us down a predestined path to fulfill a mission. Think about it—we are in our car, confined sometimes for hours, like it or not. Planning a road trip can create so much excitement. The fellowship and adventure found on a road trip is met with great preparation and anticipation. Actually, being in the car with someone for an extended length of time can be a relationship builder or destroyer.

Having to make many three- to five-hour round trips alone has made me see that a road trip is more than what merely meets the eye. Oh, it is so much more! I constantly seek to meet God on the road to Memphis, throughout Missouri, and other destinations. It is awesome to listen to songs of praise, pray, and experience the peace of God. Driving down Highway 55 or up Interstate 70, I focus on praying and seeking to know Him. There have been times when God's company had me speaking out loud, tears rolling down my face, and one hand lifted in praise. The road trips allow me to privately connect with my Lord and Savior Jesus Christ. God has us for the duration of the trip, going and coming. Can you image being in the car with someone else that no one can see and having the time of your life? Even when sleepiness creeps in, I know how to check in with family and spiritual partners. The hours tend to pass rapidly. Through God's guidance and direction, I arrive safely at my destination. God will provide direction for your journey by lighting the path. Let God be your guiding light.

My Prayer:

_____

_____

_____

_____

_____

His Voice:

_____

_____

_____

_____

_____

My Action:

_____

_____

_____

_____

_____

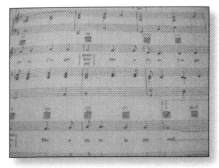

Sing Praises Unto the Lord!

*Therefore I will give thanks unto thee,
O Lord, among the heathen, and I will
sing praises unto thy name.*
—2 Samuel 22:50

Because of our nature, it takes us a while to understand the phrase, "In *all* things give thanks." It just doesn't seem right—how could I say, "Oh, thank you, Lord, for the mistakes and pain in my life." Many times I have cried naturally and in the spirit and realized that in giving God praise, even when it hurts, He makes *all* of it *all right*. It's an awesome feeling to know that whatever goes on in your life, you can go to God and He will make it bearable. There is nothing too hard for God.

God hears our every prayer and sees our every action and encounter. Remember daily that the battles that cause weakness, stress, and defeat are not ours, but the Lord's. My prayer is that we respond to every situation with Godly wisdom and act in ways that are pleasing in His sight. Overcoming the battles requires us to never get comfortable with serving the Comforter. Continue to seek higher ground and a greater anointing in the Lord.

When you go to the medical appointment, you expect the doctor to be in the office. You don't want to see the practitioner. Your concern is most important to you. So you arrive at the appointment expecting to be seen by the doctor and medicated, if necessary.

Make an appointment with God to worship Him and plead the blood of Jesus. If you make an appointment with God, you will not be disappointed. He is always there to listen and always on time. The treatment is healing and deliverance. The medicine is grace and mercy. The assurance is that in His arms you are protected. Are we charged a fee when we are no shows? Yes—heartache and pain. Make an appointment with God. Get your daily checkup to make sure you are physically, emotionally, mentally, and spiritually fit for what lies ahead.

My Prayer:

_____

_____

_____

_____

_____

His Voice:

_____

_____

_____

_____

_____

My Action:

_____

_____

_____

_____

_____

Spend the Night

*Therefore let us not sleep, as do others; but let us watch and be sober. For they that sleep; sleep in the night; and they that be drunken are drunken in the night. But let us, who are of the day, be sober, putting on the breastplate of faith and love; and for an helmet, the hope of salvation. For God hath not appointed us to wrath, but to obtain salvation by our Lord Jesus Christ.—*1 Thessalonians 5:6–9

As a little girl, I worked hard at housework. I enjoyed helping my mother by doing a lot of the cleaning around the house. Out of eight children, I know that I drove everyone mad by wanting to be clean and organized all the time. I tried hard to make sure things were picked up around the house. It was not easy with ten people living in a three bedroom house. When frustration set in from not being able to maintain order, I found myself sleeping a lot. That was my favorite pastime. My siblings say that I spent most of my days asleep. They don't mention much about me getting frustrated trying to keep the house clean by picking up after them.

As an adult, I still try to keep things organized for myself and others. The difference now is that in addition to cleaning house and sleeping, I seek to live and hear from God, have a family, and a full-time job. I realize that the devil knows that I enjoy being able to have a good night's sleep. See, the devil knows our weaknesses. Needless to say, when God calls, it's between two-thirty and four o'clock in the morning. Sometimes I find it hard to let go of the bed. We are all guilty of this act of laziness. But when I get up, I am rewarded throughout the day. Blessings flow my way, and I see the favor of God in my life. So why is it that I don't get up each time that the Lord wakes me? Is it because I allow the devil to steal what

God wants to say and do by super gluing me to the bed? God wants an opportunity to listen to us and for us to hear His voice. It is so amazing to be in the presence of the Lord during the hours that others are sleeping or partying. The devil doesn't like it when God's people are praying during the darkness of the night. If we heed the call, our lives and the lives of our loved ones will be blessed.

Knowing that many blessings from God come when I spend time kneeling in prayer, I strive to meet Him at His feet. If you are like me, you beat yourself up when you have to get up to start the day without having giving God His proper time. Praying throughout the day while you do your activities is not the same as the time spent during the night. It's like choosing a quick meal at a drive-through when you could have a five-course meal instead. When God speaks, listen to His call. When He ask you to spend the night with Him, say yes to the King and spend the day feeling like royalty.

My Prayer:

_____

_____

_____

_____

_____

His Voice:

_____

_____

_____

_____

_____

My Action:

_____

_____

_____

_____

_____

Substance Abuse

Honour the Lord with thy substance, and with the first fruits of all thine increase: So shall thy barns be filled with plenty, and thy presses shall burst out with new wine.—Proverbs 3:9–10

Substance is defined as that which has mass and occupies space. Our material possession "stuff" is substance. Our intangible belief system makes up who we are and is also considered substance. Personal substance involves character, quality of life, and material possessions. What we believe in provides substance to our characters and who we are as believers and worshipers of Christ. How do we honor the Lord with the provisions provided—our substance? Ever since I was a little girl, I thought that my substance was only my tithes of 10 percent of my earnings. Today, I realize that it is so much more.

Chemical dependency is what most people think of when the phrase substance abuse is mentioned in conversation. I believe it may be worse to be a substance abuser of the gifts and talents that God has given to each of us. The substance that God provides— possessions and talents—is to be used for His glory. When God blesses others, take notice. An enabler is defined as a person who enables another to persist in self-destructive behavior by providing excuses or making it possible to avoid pursuing the path that God has chosen for His people. God looks to others to help further His plan. Take a look around to determine if you are an abuser or an enabler of God's plan.

I immediately think about the desire to shop that I share with many. We want others to go along with us to validate our choices and excessive spending habits. Before we know it, shopping becomes a daylong event. We joyfully label ourselves as shopaholics. I sit here in tears thinking about the number of shoes and other items that I probably haven't worn in quite some time. I am also reminded of a little boy in Guatemala that asked me for a nickel. I witnessed many foreigners asking for money that my first response was to shake my head and to keep walking. As the little boy walked away, I noticed that there was no back to his worn, tattered pants. Then and now I ask God to help me to help His people with a more giving heart and godly spirit.

If I acquire and hoard an abundance of things that I place on a shelf and don't use in a manner that honors God's purpose for my life and the lives of others, I am an abuser. If I'm given charge to accomplish a task and I become complacent and wasteful, I am an abuser. If I live without thinking about the importance of tithing or the humanity of others, I am an abuser. If I enjoy luxuries and comforts with others without thinking about or providing for the less fortunate, my God-given substance might last but a season because I have allowed myself to become a substance abuser and an enabler. What are you?

My Prayer:

_____

_____

_____

_____

_____

His Voice:

_____

_____

_____

_____

_____

My Action:

_____

_____

_____

_____

_____

Day 32

The Root of Bitterness

Looking diligently lest any man fail of the grace of God; lest any root of bitterness springing up trouble you, and thereby many be defiled.—Hebrews 12:15

The root of bitterness can grow so deep within us that we begin to believe that we are justified in our negative thinking and actions toward others. There was a small little weed growing by the side of my fence. I thought cutting the weed with the weed whacker would be a simple task, so that is what I did. Within a few weeks, the weed was back. My next approach was to pull the weed up from the root. The weed popped up again. Before I knew it, the small weed was a stump about three inches thick. I couldn't pull it out or cut it with the weed whacker. It had taken a strong hold in between the steel trimming of the fence and concrete landscape. Each time I looked out the window, I thought about how sin can come into our lives and take root so strongly that we become spiritually blinded to what is really going on in our hearts and our environments.

Desperate to get rid of the symbol of how sin can take hold of our lives, I called my sister and shared the story of the weed's growth. Her suggestion was to get a product called Weed B Gon. That did not work either. The leafy stump was thicker now, and the laborious task of cutting down only took care of the problem on the surface. However, with the help of my husband, I did get to the root of the problem and destroyed the growing weed.

Think about the tiny weed that became a strong stump. Examine your thoughts, conversations, and interactions with others. So many times the root of bitterness exists because we allow it to exist and to grow in our lives and in our relationship with others. Don't allow a problem or misunderstanding to take a firm grip on your heart and mind. It reduces your ability to be productive, both naturally and spiritually. Don't allow the enemy to play the script over and over in your mind from month to month and year to year. Roots of bitterness can be passed from generation to generation. I read a quote from an unknown author that said, "Bitterness is hindrance, but when it is discovered its noxious roots have spread and it springs up as something much bigger and more destructive."

Forgiveness, along with love and kindness, destroys the root of bitterness. Holding on to hurtful situations takes up room that God can use to deposit blessings. Christ died so that we might be free to live an abundant and glorious life. Forgive quickly and be set free. The Bible says, "If the Son therefore shall make you free, ye shall be free indeed" (John 8:36). Your freedom is in your ability to forgive.

My Prayer:

_____

_____

_____

_____

_____

His Voice:

_____

_____

_____

_____

_____

My Action:

_____

_____

_____

_____

_____

Day 33

Thoughts of Peace

For my thoughts are not your thoughts, neither are your ways my ways, saith the Lord.—Isaiah 55:8

What are your thoughts today, at this moment? We all have issues that may be pressing heavily on us. The flesh has us thinking all the time about one thing or another. It could be our finances, health, relationships, family, or our jobs. We can very easily let our thoughts and sinful worrying consume us and take away our energy and ability to be productive in our daily lives. When we are unproductive, we are of no use to anyone, including ourselves. We are just going through the motions.

What I love about God's Word is the comfort He expresses in Jeremiah 29:11. He affirms us by saying, "For I know the thoughts that I think toward you, saith the LORD, thoughts of peace, and not of evil, to give you an expected end." It really doesn't matter what we are going through because God has given us His Word. When God gives us His Word, it is so much more than someone saying, "You have my word; I promise I am going to do it." When God gives us His Word, He is giving us His love. God wants us to find comfort in knowing Him. Through the Holy Spirit we have tranquility and security. No harm can come to us, even when the devil has access to us, because God has given us His promise of an expected end, which is always better than the way we think things will turn out. God gives us strength to be tested and tried so that He can receive His glory from our prayers and praise.

When we think that we can't go any further in our situations, and we are ready to throw in the towel, we must remember that God never fails. A promise is a promise. Remember God lets us know that He is, "able to do exceeding abundantly above all that we ask or think, according to the power that worketh in us" (Ephesians 3:20). Believe that God's Word is His bond of love through the shedding of Christ's blood on Calvary. Keep your thoughts aligned with God's thinking about you, and expect the unexpected.

My Prayer:

_____

_____

_____

_____

_____

His Voice:

_____

_____

_____

_____

_____

My Action:

_____

_____

_____

_____

_____

True Love

And now abideth faith, hope, charity, these three; but the greatest of these is charity.—1 Corinthians 13:13

ctions really do speak louder than words. God speaks to us through the Holy Spirit and the written word. He gives us His promises and reinforces them with the statement, "He is not a man that He should lie." More than just words, God gave His beloved son Jesus Christ so that we might have life and live more abundantly. What love! God's love is worthy of a daily celebration. While Valentine's Day is a commercial celebration designed for lovers, true believers recognize true love everyday, which is Jesus Christ, every day. If you are without a mate, stand firm and know that you are loved by the Master every day, not just one day in the year. A lot is spent unnecessarily on material things to show love on Valentine's Day, but what happens the day after? No other lover can lay down his life in humble submission and then repeatedly, without a second thought, stand ready and waiting to watch over us. True love comes from following and believing in God for God is Love.

Paul instructs us the way of love in 1 Corinthians 13:1–13. The passage is presented with the word charity replaced with the word love:

> "Though I speak with the tongues of men and of angels, and have not love, I am become as sounding brass, or a tinkling cymbal. And though I have the gift of prophecy, and understand all mysteries, and all knowledge; and though I have all faith, so that I could remove mountains, and have not love, I am nothing. And though I bestow all my goods to feed the poor, and though I give my body to be burned, and have not love, it profiteth me nothing. Love suffereth long, and is kind; love envieth not; love vaunteth not itself, is not puffed up, Doth not behave itself unseemly, seeketh not her own, is not easily provoked, thinketh no evil; Rejoiceth not in iniquity, but rejoiceth in

the truth; Beareth all things, believeth all things, hopeth all things, endureth all things. Love never faileth: but whether there be prophecies, they shall fail; whether there be tongues, they shall cease; whether there be knowledge, it shall vanish away. For we know in part, and we prophesy in part. But when that which is perfect is come, then that which is in part shall be done away. When I was a child, I spake as a child, I understood as a child, I thought as a child: but when I became a man, I put away childish things. For now we see through a glass, darkly; but then face to face: now I know in part; but then shall I know even as also I am known. And now abideth faith, hope, love, these three; but the greatest of these is love."

Lord, help us to clearly see your love and compassion for us. Forgive us when we have self-pity, doubt, and depression due to a failed relationship. Help us in our relationships with others and strengthen our loving relationships with you.

My Prayer:

_____

_____

_____

_____

_____

His Voice:

_____

_____

_____

_____

_____

My Action:

_____

_____

_____

_____

_____

Tug of War

For the weapons of our warfare are not carnal, but mighty through God to the pulling down of strongholds.—2 Corinthians 10:4

Tug of war is a sport that directly pits two teams against each other in a test of strength. It has been around for ages and was part of the Olympic Games from 1900 to 1920. Two teams struggle to keep the rope's centered flag on their side of the line and eventually pull the opposing team over. This display of strength is a triumphant victory for one of the teams.

So many times over the past few days I have experienced that tug of war in the workplace, home, and mind as I seek to spend time to be closer to God. What causes us to allow God to be pulled away from the center of our lives as we seek to develop a close relationship with Him? I realize it isn't enough for me to stay in the center. The center is a good place if we are in the center of His will or trying to find a place of balance in our lives. We must seek to draw nearer to God. When we draw neigh to God, he promises to draw neigh to us (James 4:8). Continue to see the invisible tug of war in your day and pull closer to God. Strive to eliminate those things that pull you away for God's plan for your life. Know the opposing team and remember it is in direct opposition to where you want to be with God and His plan for your life.

Today, dig your heels in, get a stronger grip, and pull toward God's plan for your life. Who's on your team? Make connections with spiritually-minded people. God promises that you can; negativity comes from the opposition. Remember in wartime, there is strength in numbers. "Where one or two are gathered together in His name, there He is also" (Matthew 18:20).

My Prayer:

_____

_____

_____

_____

_____

His Voice:

_____

_____

_____

_____

_____

My Action:

_____

_____

_____

_____

_____

Walking in the Rain

The Lord shall open unto thee his good treasure, the heaven to give the rain unto thy land in his season, and to bless all the work of thine hand: and thou shalt lend unto many nations, and thou shalt not borrow.—Deuteronomy 28:12

Each morning I give God thanks for allowing me to see another day. One particular morning, I looked out the window to behold the beauty of the Lord. As I left the window to bow down on my knees to pray, I heard the voice of the Lord say, "It is raining." I hurried to put on the proper shoes to go outside to walk and pray. This would be the day that I put my thoughts into action. I had always thought about leisurely walking in the rain unprotected but never ventured out. Naturally, we seek shelter from the rain.

When we ask God to rain on us, we must be ready to get wet. Being caught in the rain is different from going out in the rain and saying, "Rain on me." On my walk, I found myself speaking to the rain, wind, and God. If the rain slackened, I would say, "Lord, I am out here. Send more rain. I need the rain." I noticed that the trees shielded me from the rain. I immediately moved to the center of the road where there were no trees and more rain coming down. This particular morning, I felt if I didn't feel the natural rain, then I wasn't feeling the spiritual rain. I wanted to be rained on.

When we are walking with the Lord, we are more protected than when we walk on a natural path. The heavy rain should not cause us to run for cover. We must give God continuous praise for His shield of protection. If we don't feel the rain, we are not on the right path. Praying for more rain pleases God. As I continued my natural/spiritual walk, I felt one heavy drop in the center of my head. God reminded me to stay in the center of His will. You may be wondering if any cars came as I walked down the center of the road. Yes, as in life, potential trouble will come. But you press on. I moved to the right. When difficult situations come into your life,

God wants you to know which way to move, even if the move causes you to stand still. I moved over for the cars and cars moved over for me.

There are benefits of walking with God. See an outpouring of rain in your life by thanking God for His many blessings. God needs more people to walk with Him in their daily lives. Salvation is an individual walk. When you look back at how far you have come in your walk, thank God for His blessings. Let God rain on you and pour out His Holy Spirit in your life!

My Prayer:

_____

_____

_____

_____

_____

His Voice:

_____

_____

_____

_____

My Action:

_____

_____

_____

_____

_____

When I Am Weak

Therefore, I take pleasure in infirmities, in reproaches, in necessities, in persecutions, in distresses for Christ's sake; for when I am weak, then am I strong.
—2 Corinthians 12:10

What lies within us is more than what we can see, feel, or think. God has given us the ability to achieve in areas that we feel the most incompetent. Realizing the strength that lies within is so hard to do. The great implant that was given to us by God at birth equips us with inner strength. Strength in weakness is only evoked and realized when we strive to accomplish the will of God in all of our endeavors.

Working as a principal in an elementary school, I felt intimidated on so many levels. Now I realize that God used my feeling of inadequacy to display service, compassion, and humility. While completing my doctoral program, I admit that I truly felt a fine line between sane and insane. Now I realize that my frailty of mind or stress was God's way of increasing my faith, establishing prayer and worship practices, and intensifying a relationship with Him. Now I find myself asking again, "Lord, strengthen me to handle the situations and do the things that you have placed before me." When we get to the point where we can thank the Lord for the distresses as well as the blessings that come our way, we will truly feel the power of God giving us strength to make it each step of the way because it is really not about us.

I am continually learning to see it as joyful when things don't go the way that I think that they should. I ask what is to be learned from this experience. Learn to take something from each day to provide food for thought and strength for tomorrow. Our stripes can't compare to those endured by Christ Jesus. Each time we face adversity in our lives, we must know that during our weakest moments, God comes to give us strength for the journey.

Remember that God's strength is peaceful and quiet. It allows us to walk in the faith and hope of His promises. Our weaknesses come to make us stronger. Through the exercises of prayer and praise, you will gain strength. Paul said when he prayed, the Lord spoke to him and said, "My grace is sufficient for thee: for my strength is made perfect in weakness" (2 Corinthians 12:9). If you are doing everything that you know to please God, He will whisper to you that your strength is in your weakness.

My Prayer:

_____

_____

_____

_____

_____

His Voice:

_____

_____

_____

_____

_____

My Action:

_____

_____

_____

_____

_____

Wish Them Well!

Beloved, I wish above all things that thou mayest prosper *and be in health, even as thy soul prospereth.*—3 John 2

J ohn wrote well wishes to his friend. It can be most difficult for us to wish our enemies well with sincerity, meekness, and a God-like spirit. Wishing well to those who are indifferent to us conditions our hearts to be more Christlike. To some, it is the same as turning the other cheek and maybe just as painful, but it must be done. By wishing them well, we have not only asked God to look after our enemies, but to take care of them naturally and spiritually! What greater blessings can one bestow upon another individual? By wishing everyone well, animosity is eliminated and we become humble and better able to serve others and work for the Master.

Not so long ago, I believed that "wishing someone well" was just a saying that did not have much depth or sincerity. I would gravitate toward "God bless you," or "I will be praying for you." I simply felt wishing someone well was not putting God first. Now I see the power in the words around the wish—the focus is to make sure that it is powered by the Holy Spirit!

In today's world, a wish often lacks the power that comes from faith in God. It is the compassion, belief, and love of God we strive to convey in our words of hope for others that make the difference. Wishing others well not only helps to encourage, it can change the behavior of the receiver of the message and evoke inner peace within the sender.

My Prayer:

_____

_____

_____

_____

_____

His Voice:

_____

_____

_____

_____

_____

My Action:

_____

_____

_____

_____

_____

Day 39

Wrestling Match

And he said, Let me go, for the day breaketh. And he said, I will not let thee go, except thou bless me.—Genesis 32:26

Situations in life demand that we remain ready for spiritual warfare. Difficult tests are won in the spiritual realm. Wrestling with the enemy requires constant fasting and praying to gain the victory. Never give up on prayer and reading the Word of God. When you get to the point of saying, "There is nothing else I can do," remember there is still one thing that can be done. It requires more energy, commitment, and will power. It is focused praying, which takes a real commitment and dedication to pray until something happens. This prayer can leave you physically exhausted and spiritually renewed.

Think about Jacob. When morning came, Jacob emerged with a glorious limp. He had been in the presence of God all night. Jacob did not give up. He struggled for his blessing. Jacob really did not care if it took all night (see Genesis 32:24–31). We have to continue to stay before God to receive His blessings. Whatever you have brought before the Lord, don't give up. When others think you are down for the count, continue in prayer, and believe God rewards those that diligently seek Him.

Through continued effectual and fervent prayer, Jacob obtained the favor of God by staying the course and praying, even though he was worn out from his struggle to gain a blessing from God. Imagine yourself in a prayer-filled wrestling match getting knocked, thrown, punched, and sometimes kicked about. Because you stayed the course, you leave the ring helplessly exhausted but spiritually renewed. Stay in the ring to receive the blessings of the Lord.

My Prayer:

_____

_____

_____

_____

_____

His Voice:

_____

_____

_____

_____

My Action:

_____

_____

_____

_____

Yes, Lord!

For if I do this thing willingly, I have a reward: but if against my will, a dispensation of the gospel is committed unto me.—1 Corinthians 9:17

Saying yes to the Lord is so different from saying yes to anyone that you can know in life. When you say yes to the Lord, you know the breath, height and depth of who God really is on an even higher level. Saying yes diminishes the opponent of yes, which is no. Saying yes puts us in alignment with God's will for our lives.

A phrase from the song, Completely Yes says, "From the bottom of my heart my soul says yes Lord, completely, yes Lord." Letting the song play in your mind solidifies it in your spirit and brings forth a high praise to worship Him. "Yes, Lord" is the answer to God's will for your life. If the voice of the Lord sends you to help someone that has wronged you, it's "Yes, Lord." If the Lord says turn right instead of left, it's "Yes, Lord." If the Lord says be quiet, wait, stop, go, pray, it's "Yes, Lord." Even when we are in turmoil, it's "Yes, Lord, completely, yes, Lord."

Saying yes to the Lord is an act of obedience and submissiveness. Responding to the voice of the Lord with yes releases God's favor upon our lives. The awesomeness of God is that He knows. He is El Roi, a God who sees all things. But He also needs and wants us. God uses ordinary people to spread His Word and proclaim the gospel of Christ. Can you image a God that is so great that He wants and needs you? There is no time for an answer of maybe, later, or tomorrow. If you are not willing to say, "Yes, I will be used by you, Lord. Yes, I will acknowledge Jesus Christ as your son," then God can't use you and He moves on to someone who is willing to say yes. Say "Yes, Lord," and watch God enter into your life and the lives of your family members. Today, be the difference that you were looking for yesterday.

My Prayer:

_____

_____

_____

_____

_____

His Voice:

_____

_____

_____

_____

_____

My Action:

_____

_____

_____

_____

_____

A Place of Your Own to Give God Glory

(Use the following note pages to record your personal experiences with God and to continue to give Him glory).

Notes:

Notes:

Notes:

Notes:

Notes:

About the Author

Gwendolyn Wilson Diggs believes in mustard seed faith by praying powerfully and maintaining a strong relationship with God. Listening to His voice and striving to do His will is her constant endeavor. Spreading His Word and proclaiming the gospel of Christ is her passion as she strives to encourage others to strengthen their walk with Christ. Her only regret is if she had practiced sincerely calling on His name when she was younger that she would have more time to satisfy the intense hunger and thirsting for His word. She is a member of Mt. Calvary Church of God In Christ in East St. Louis, Illinois.

She holds a Doctorate in Educational Leadership from Nova Southeastern University in Ft. Lauderdale, Florida, M.S degree in Education Administration from the University of Missouri Saint Louis, and a B.S. degree in Business Management from Nova Southeastern University in Ft. Lauderdale, Florida. Dr. Diggs is the Assistant Superintendent of Elementary Education in the Ferguson-Florissant School District in Florissant, Missouri.

Born in Memphis, Tennessee, she now resides in Florissant, Missouri, with her husband, Darryl. She is the praying mother of three adult children, Darryl Jr., Jordan, and Ardella.

Blessed are they which do hunger and thirst after
righteousness; for they shall be filled. Matthew 5:6

Contact the Author:

Email: aplaceofmyown@att.net

Telephone: 314-265-4934

References

Blandly, Ernest W. and Norris, John S., *Where He Leads Me* (#360), 1890. Publisher Unknown.

Crouch, Sandra. Completely Yes. *Classic Gold: We're Waiting*, 2003. Light Records, compact disc 4:01.

Holy Bible: The Kings James Study Bible. (previously published as The Liberty Annotated study Bible, The Annotated Study Bible), King James Version, 1988. Nashville: Thomas Nelson Publishers.

The New Britannica-Webster Dictionary and Reference Guide, s.v. "Specializes."